WRITTEN BY LOUISE WRIGHT PRICE
ILLUSTRATED BY BENJAMIN REID PHILLIPS

copyright © 2020 Louise Wright Price
All rights reserved.
No part of this book may be reproduced,
except for purposes of review,
without written permission of the publisher.

Dedicated to
The Man Himself

(1892-1931)
Charlie Poole

And also to my father, Warren S. Wright, who instilled in me a love for Charlie's music, and to my mother, Ellie B. Wright, who loved any music as long as it had 'pep.'

There once was a fellow named Charlie Poole who just loved to play the banjo. In fact, he learned to play his banjo when he wasn't but about seven or eight years old.

Charlie Poole

Back when Charlie was little, a lot of children his age weren't allowed to go to school, but were sent to work in the mills so they could help their families buy groceries and things they needed. Charlie was one of these children, and so he grew up not knowing how to read or write. But he knew how to play that banjo – really well.

Young Mill Workers

After Charlie got grown, he moved to a town in North Carolina called Spray (they merged Spray with two other towns later on – Leaksville and Draper – and now it's called Eden). He went to work in another textile mill – Spray Cotton Mills – but he kept playing that banjo.

Spray Cotton Mills

In Spray, he met a lot of other really good musicians. Two of the best were Posey Rorer – he played fiddle – and Norman Woodlieff – he played guitar.

Charlie decided to form a band with Posey and Norman, and they called themselves the North Carolina Ramblers. And they did ramble! They rambled all over the country making music and making a big name for themselves. People loved to watch them play!

Working in a mill back then was really hard work, and the pay wasn't too good – just a few dollars a week. Charlie got the idea that they should go to New York and audition to make a record. The three of them went into the mill one morning, played a tune for the workers there, and then announced – "Goodbye boys, we're gone!" And off they went, to the big city of New York, marching up to the offices of Columbia Records and announcing that they were there to make a record.

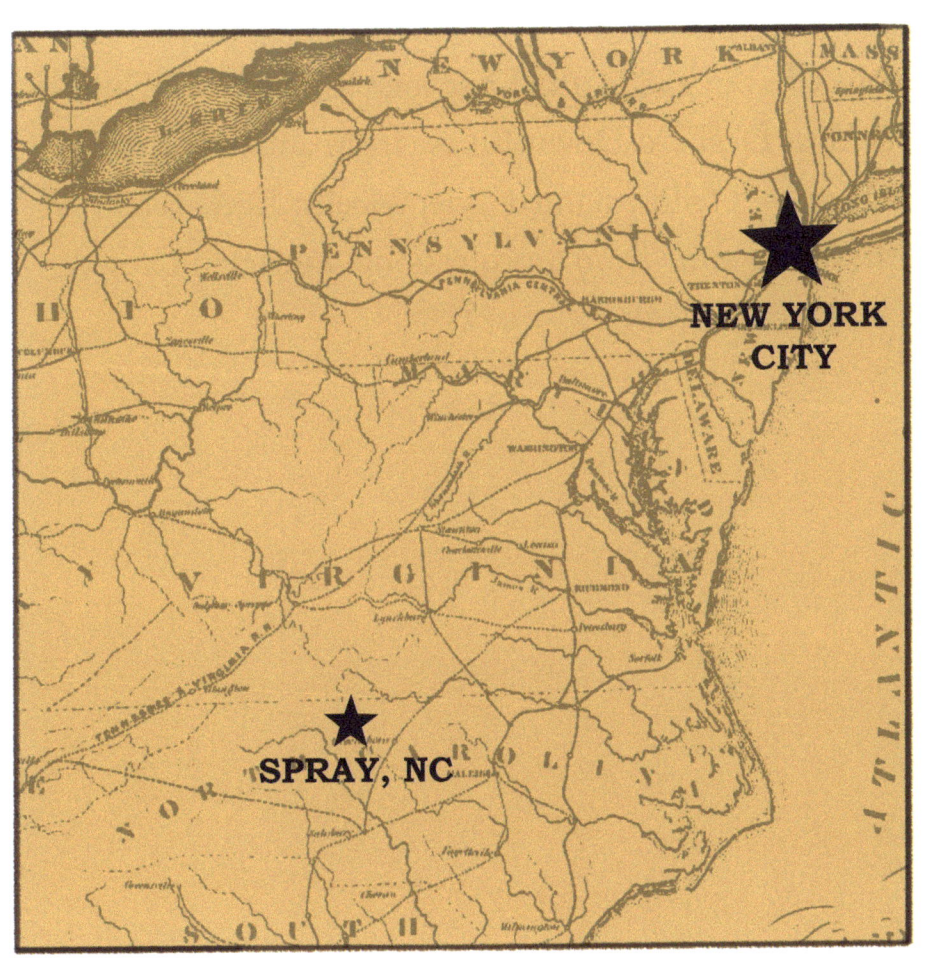

Spray to New York

Now, Charlie had learned a special tune called "Don't Let Your Deal Go Down Blues" from another musician in Spray – a fellow named Tyler Meeks. And, Tyler had learned the tune from a professional musician named Charlie Blackstock.

The thing about so many of these good musicians – most all of them learned to play their banjos and fiddles and guitars when they were little children – they wanted to play so bad! Anyway, they had learned to play so well, that Columbia recorded them right away, and that very tune – nicknamed "The Deal" – became a smash hit, outselling anything else at the time. Charlie and his band became big stars!

Charlie continued to record tunes, even though his band would change. Roy Harvey replaced Norman Woodlieff on guitar, and Lonnie Austin replaced Posey Rorer on fiddle.

Even more musicians were added on later recordings, notably Lucy Terry on piano.

And Charlie learned something important – Charlie's loving wife, Lou Emma, taught Charlie how to read and write so he could sign his record contracts. It's never too late to learn.

Lou Emma Rorer Poole

Even though the band members might change, their sound never did – Charlie made sure everything sounded just the way he wanted it to. And that sound wasn't like anything anyone had heard before. It was modern music for a new time in America. Musicians even today still talk about Charlie Poole, and they even try to sound like him. But there was only one Charlie Poole, and his music will always live on.

LOUISE WRIGHT PRICE is President of Piedmont Folk Legacies, Inc., a non-profit whose mission is to "promote and preserve the musical and cultural legacy of the Piedmont region and to celebrate its influence on the development of American vernacular music, as exemplified by Charlie Poole." Along with Marianne S. Aiken, she founded the Charlie Poole Music Festival in 1996. In 2019, Louise conceived the PICK (Piedmont Instrument Classes for Kids) program to provide elementary school students with instruction in traditional instruments and educate them about the rich cultural heritage of the Piedmont region. An avid preservationist, she was a 2016 recipient of the Preservation North Carolina Gertrude S. Carraway Award of Merit.

BENJAMIN REID PHILLIPS is a sequential artist and illustrator whose work has been featured in the Cartoon Art Museum's Monsters of Webcomics series, anthologies from Fantagraphics Books, Top Shelf Comics, Midnight Horizons Press and The Savannah College of Art and Design. He won the Georgia College Press Association's Best Editorial Feature for his District serial, Dr. Dead. Phillips worked on Devil's Due comic edition of FOX's hit TV series, "Family Guy" and created storyboards for the film "A Promise."

He is the co-author of "Storyboarding Essentials SCAD Creative Essentials (How to Translate Your Story to the Screen for Film, TV, and Other Media)" from Watson Guptill.

Phillips is currently a Professor of Foundation Studies at the Savannah College of Art and Design.

SHARON TONGBUA is a graphic designer from Eden, NC who has provided design services to many businesses and organizations in the area for over 40 years. Ms. Tongbua prepared the layout of this book and designed its cover.

The photo of Charlie Poole is courtesy of Kinney Rorrer. We are indebted to Kinney for his tireless efforts to document and promote the important legacy of this enduring musical legend, especially in his important biography "Rambling Blues: The Life & Songs of Charlie Poole."